the Xceedingly funny joke book

Dyslexia Institute
Illustrated by Bill Piggins

WALKER BOOKS
LONDON

What is dyslexia?

Dyslexia affects about one in every twenty-five people – that's one child in every classroom.

In order to be able to read, write, spell and do number work effectively a child has to combine all the individual skills of learning into the one complex skill of being able to read and write accurately. A dyslexic child has specific learning difficulties which obstruct the organization of the individual skills.

To illustrate what this means, imagine a filing cabinet containing hundreds of papers, filed in individual slots but without labels. So when specific information is sought, it is impossible to find that information because it is not organized properly.

Being dyslexic is rather like this: in the same way that a filing cabinet needs to be organized and labelled by the person who is to use it, so too does the learning system for a dyslexic.

This is why it is essential that dyslexics should be recognized and helped when they are young enough – before they start to fail and lose confidence in themselves. If they are not given that appropriate help they will almost certainly under-achieve in school and probably in later life.

Dyslexics have difficulties, but they also have abilities. Many of them have creative talents and are potential actors, architects, artists, computer and electronic experts, designers, engineers, entrepreneurs. They have a different kind of learning ability. If they can't learn the way they are being taught, then they must be taught the way they can learn.

What is the Dyslexia Institute?

The Dyslexia Institute was established in 1972 to ensure the identification and teaching of dyslexics and the training of their teachers, and to offer advice and further people's knowledge about dyslexia. It is the only national network in the world offering this range of help.

Since the Dyslexia Institute first began teaching, it has developed learning programmes to build the organization of skills into a learning process for each student. Firstly individual weaknesses and abilities are assessed, then a structured teaching programme is designed which involves memory training, exercises to correct specific weaknesses in auditory and visual perception and in hand skills. By building a cumulative structure of learning geared to the individual student's needs, their confidence will improve and they will cope with learning in school.

Dyslexia affects people irrespective of background or intelligence, and provision is costly. The Dyslexia Foundation Bursary Fund was established in 1981 to ensure that those needing help should not be denied it.

The royalties from this book will go to the Dyslexia Foundation Bursary Fund.

A letter from Susan Hampshire

I think the most important step for youngsters with specific learning difficulties today is to be properly assessed as soon as possible and then have expert specialist teaching. That is why the Bursary Fund is so vital. Many parents who are not able to pay for these lessons can call on the Bursary Fund which supports 150 students (more if their coffers are full) to subsidize their child's lessons and thus prepare them to face the future with hope.

Over the years I have travelled up and down the country to the various Dyslexia Institutes and met many children, some when they have only just been assessed. At this stage the children have been withdrawn, lacking in confidence and too shy to talk to me. When visiting that same centre six months later the same children come bouncing up with smiling faces, full of confidence, to tell me of their progress. The change is so overwhelming that I know the special teaching offered by the Dyslexia Institute is the key to dyslexic children having a happy, fulfilled life.

Sadly there are still many children needing help at the Dyslexia Institute's 20 centres and 49 outposts or in 41 school centres, and regrettably there is not enough money to subsidize them. The need is so enormous; money runs out more quickly than it comes in. It is heartbreaking to think of the children who would be helped if only the resources were available. Lack of money is coming between them and the future they deserve.

Susan Hampshire
Patron of the Dyslexia Institute Bursary Fund

The Xceedingly funny joke book

These jokes were collected from pupils at Dyslexia Institutes throughout the country, with the addition of contributions from celebrities.

The collection was originally privately produced by the Derby Dyslexia Institute, and is now available nationally to raise proceeds for the Dyslexia Foundation Bursary Fund.

Contents

PEOPLE

Why does Batman carry worms?
To feed Robin.
Jonathan Grant, 9, Lincoln

What do you get if a huge hairy monster steps on Batman and Robin?
Flatman and Ribbon.
Jamie Whatshott, 7, Lincoln

What do you call a woman with 2 toilets?
Lulu!
H. Denshan, Newcastle upon Tyne

What do you call Postman Pat when he's on the dole?
Pat.
James Cundall, Wilmslow / Nick, 15, Leicester / Robert Bretville, 11, Sutton Coldfield

D.H.S.S. UB40 CARD
PAT

People

☆ "During the Election Campaign of 1987, there were times when I got a little depressed, especially as the weather in Derbyshire always seemed to be wet. But as we entered a Village Hall in the closing days of the campaign, I thought the tide was turning. A little old lady in a sodden mackintosh, nose streaming, came up to me. "Mrs. Currie," she said, "I've got a present for you!" and she stood up on tiptoe and gave me a big kiss. "Well thank you," I said, much cheered up. "Oh no, you won't thank me," she countered with a grin, "cause I'm Labour, and I've got flu!"

Rt. Hon. Edwina Currie M.P.

☆ What do you call a woman who is sitting at a revolving wheel, with wet clay in her hands, and four pints of beer on her head?
Beatrix Potter.

Rt. Hon. Neil Kinnock M.P.

the Xceedingly funny joke book

What's the difference between a prison warder and a watch seller?

One watches cells - the other sells watches!

Sarie-Marais Hearnon, 9, Grantham

☆ Why did the Mexican push his wife off the cliff?

Tequila!

Mark Curry

What do you call a Judge who has no thumbs?

Justice Fingers!

Philip Treace, 15, Nottingham

A man went into a shop and asked if he could have a camouflage jacket. The shop assistant replied, "Sorry sir, but I can't find them!"

R.X. Merritt, Cleveland

What are 2 robbers called?

A pair of nickers!

Jonathan Martland, 16, Stone

What does the Spanish farmer say to his chickens?

"Oh lay!"

Stephen Percy, Winchester

A Chinese man complained to the Tourist board that it was impossible to ride his bicycle between the double yellow lines!

Andrew Cunning, 13, Princethorpe College

What's pink, all wrinkly and belongs to Grandma?

Grandpa!

R. Exton, 10, Grantham

What did the policeman say to his tummy?
"You're under a vest!"
Andrew Fu, 7, Wilmslow

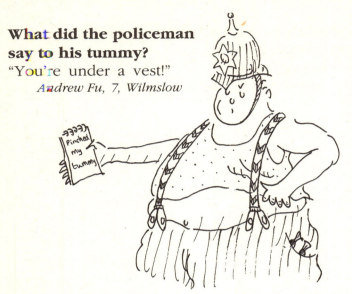

A man wanted to hire a horse so he went to a priest who gave him a horse but warned him, "The horse only obeys these instructions - it's 'Alleluya' to STOP and 'Thank the Lord' to GO." The man set off on the horse saying, "Thank the Lord, Thank the Lord." The horse went faster and faster, then the man saw they were approaching a cliff edge! He was trying to think of the word to stop and just 5cms from the edge he remembered and said "Alleluya!" The horse stopped. The relieved man shouted in joy, "Thank the Lord!"
Wendy Barton, 12, Bolton

Why did the man with one hand cross the road?

To get to the second hand shop!

Toby Milburn, 14, Stone,
G. Woodcock, 10, Wilmslow

Why shouldn't you believe a person who tells you something when they're asleep?

Because they're lying!

Simon Barker, 8, Wilmslow

A man on a building site was laying bricks. Suddenly a saw fell from the planks above and chopped off his ear. "Ow, where's my ear?" yelled the man. "Here it is, I've found it," said his mate. The first man said, "That's not MY ear, mine had a pencil behind it!"

Philip Harper, 12, Birkenhead

What happened to Ray when he was stepped on by an elephant?

He became an ex-Ray!

Finlay McNab, 9, Fairfield School,
Loughborough

☆ A Yorkshireman lost his wife, went to see the Stonemason and said, "I just want a simple inscription on the gravestone - 'She was thine'." The Stonemason said, "It'll be ready next week." Next week the man goes to see the gravestone and there is the inscription - "She was thin" . He said, "No, no, no - you've missed out the 'e'." The Stonemason said, "Of course, don't worry, I'll put it right before the stone's put in place." The next week the stone's in place and the widower goes to see it. On it is the inscription "E she was thin".

Roy Hudd

Executioner : Do you have one last request?
Prisoner : Yes, can I sing a song?
Executioner : Why not! Yes, carry on.
Prisoner : Ten million green bottles hanging on the wall...!

Philip Hodson, 12, Wilmslow

"Mummy, Mummy, there's a man at the door with a bill!"
"Don't be silly, dear, it's a duck with a hat on."

James Hadfield, 9,
St. Crispins' Prep. School, Leicester

☆ **Two drunks on a London Underground train.**
1st Drunk : Is this Wembley?
2nd Drunk : No, it's Thursday.
1st Drunk : So am I, let's have another drink!

Simon Williams

Two Irishmen were looking for a job when they saw a sign :
"Tree Fellers Wanted".
One said to the other, "Now look at that! Sure it's a pity there's only 2 of us!"

Ian Hecks, 11

What do you call a man with a car on his head?
Jack.

What do you call a man with a spade in his head?
Doug.

What do you call a man without a spade in his head?
Dougless.

Anna Jamieson, 10, Nottingham,
Stephen, 14, Leicester

"Simon - can you spell your name backwards?"
"No mis."

Jonathan Lewis

There's a man playing darts. He throws
twice and scores 2 double 20s. His last dart
hits a nun sitting at a nearby table. The
scorer yells, "One nun dead and eighty!"

Gareth Woodcock, 10, Wilmslow

How can you see flying saucers?

Trip the waiter up.

Nicolas Huyg, 9,
Foremarke Hall, Repton Prep. School

An Englishman, another Englishman and an American were on the top of a skyscraper. The American said, "If you jump off the top of here, you can bounce off the clouds and land back again on here."

One of the Englishmen said, "Go on then." The American does this, and he bounces off the clouds gracefully and lands back on the skyscraper! The other Englishman decides to have a go. He jumps off the top, plunges through the clouds and goes "SPLAT!" on the sidewalk below.

The remaining Englishman turns to the American and says, "Oh Superman, you can be really mean at times!"

Daniel Thompson,
12, Harrogate

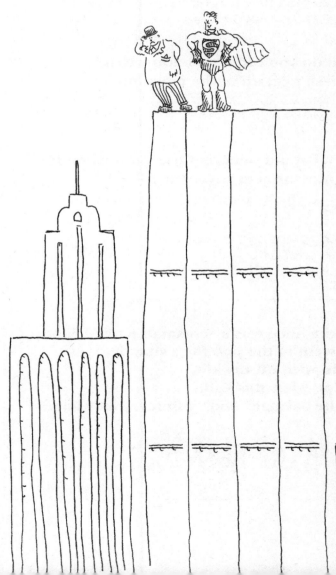

Why did the girl put her guitar in the deep freeze?
So she could play it cool!
Philip Tuckwell, 10, Derby

What do you call a skeleton when it doesn't get up in the morning?
Lazybones.
Analie Sarson, 11

What did General Custer say when the Indians came over the hill?
"Oh no, here come the Indians!"
Graeme Carter, 13, Altrincham

☆ **There once was a Scotsman named Sandy,**
Who went to the pub for a shandy,
He whipped off his kilt,
To wipe what was spilt,
And the barmaid said, "Blimey, that's handy!"
Leslie Crowther

Leslie Crowther

Why was Cinderella knocked out of the football team?

Because she kept running away from the ball.

Adam Gardner, 7,
Horwich Centre, Bolton

Who was the first underwater spy?

James Pond.

Kevin Portess, 11, Scunthorpe

Why do Scotsmen have double glazing?

So their kids don't hear the ice–cream van!

Ben McFadzean, 12, Coventry

the Xceedingly funny joke book

☆ **Real life story from Beryl Reid.**

"The summer before last, on a very hot day, I had had a few of my great friends to lunch. We had eaten a lot, and also had rather a lot to drink. When they left at about 3.30 in the afternoon, I took all my clothes off and fell fast asleep on top of my bed. I woke up later to find a printed note through my letterbox saying 'Your windows have been cleaned' - I think this rather got about the village!"
Beryl Reid

"May I go swimming, Mummy?"
"No, you can't. There are sharks there."
"But Daddy's swimming."
"He's insured."
Matthew Simpson, 12, Sutton Coldfield

☆ **Man on top of a cliff at "Lover's Leap". He's looking over the edge to the rocks beneath shouting, "Sorry Ethel - I've chickened out!"**
Felicity Kendal

ANIMALS

How does an octopus go into battle?
Well-armed!
David Bradley, 11, Foremarke Hall, Repton Prep. School

Who doesn't know his lefts from his rights?
A dyslexic octopus.
David Robins, 9, Northampton

What do you call a bear without an ear?
B-
A. Cross, Newcastle upon Tyne

What do you call a fly with no wings?
A walk!
L. Cooper, Darlington

Animals

An Englishman, an Irishman and a Scotsman were on a train. They passed a cow. The Englishman said, "That's an English cow." The Irishman said, "No, it's an Irish cow." The Scotsman said, "No, it's a Scottish cow - it's got bagpipes under it!"

Iain McArthur, 12, Stone

What do you get if you pour boiling water down a rabbit hole?

Hot cross bunnies!

Damien Hall, Oldham

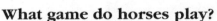

What game do horses play?

Stable tennis!

Anne Macdougall, 9, Glasgow

What's Rupert the Bear's middle name?

The!

Hazel, 11, Darlington

Two teddy bears in the airing cupboard, which one was in the army?
The one on the tank!
Jane Quincey, 10, Lincoln

Why do polar bears wear fur coats?
Because they'd look silly in plastic macs!
James Hall, Oldham,
Richard Hawkins, 8, Winchester

☆ **Have you heard about Arthur the "Human Chameleon", who died of exhaustion after crawling over a tartan rug?**
Victoria Wood

Victoria Wood.

Animals

Why did the monkey fall out of the tree?
Because it was dead.
Why did the other monkey fall out of the tree?
Because it was stapled to the dead one!
A. Cross, Newcastle upon Tyne

How does a monkey cook his toast?
On a gorilla!
Christopher Hobden, 13, Tonbridge

☆ **What do you call a monkey with a machine gun?**
Sir!
Bill Buckley

What do baby apes sleep in?
Apricots!
*A. Cross, Newcastle upon Tyne,
Philip Wing, 9, Bletchingley*

What's a horse's favourite T.V. programme?
"Neighbours"!
Andrew McMahon, 8, Lichfield

What lies 100 feet in the air?
A centipede in bed!
Scott Hall, Oldham

Why are there no anadin in the jungle?
Because the parrots...eat'em...all! (Think about it!)
Fian Andrews, Nottingham

Why are parrots clever?
They suck-seed!
Vanessa Marsden, 11, Sheffield

What do you get if you cross a kangaroo with an elephant?
Big holes in Australia
David Higham, 12, Bolton,
John Ford, 12, Bletchingly

Why can't you milk a mouse?
Because you can't get a bucket under it!
Sarah Buckley, 12, Loughborough

What do you do with a wasp that is ill?
Send it to a wospital!
Ritchie Morgan, 7, Eversley/Staines

Why did the germ cross the microscope?
To get to the other slide!
Richard Caines, 10, Horwich Centre, Bolton

What do you call a baby crab?
A nippet!
J. Appleby, Newcastle upon Tyne

the Xceedingly funny joke book

Why did the dinosaur cross the road?
Because the chicken hadn't been invented!
Jonathan Davies, 10, Solihull/Coventry

How do frogs die?
They Kermit suicide!
Peter Clarke, 11, Sheffield

What's black and dangerous and sits in a tree?
A blackbird with a machine gun!
Andrew Scantlebury, 10, Altrincham

What is a sleeping bull called?
A bulldozer.
Paul Woodcraft, 10, Sheffield

What is the wettest animal?
A reindeer!
Kevin Dempster, 10, Stone

What would happen if pigs could fly?
The price of bacon would go up!
Giles Cooper, 15, Repton School!

Animals

Man : "What have you got in that sack, farmer?"
Farmer : "Fish."
Man : "If I can guess how many fish you have in that sack, can I have one?"
Farmer : "If you can guess how many fish there are, you can have both of them."
  Ross Bennett, 13, Derby

What animal gets bigger when you take something away?
A fox when you take away the "f".
  Iain Wright, 11, Sevenoaks

How did bulldogs get such flat noses?
From chasing parked cars!
  Emma Smith, 12, Sutton Coldfield

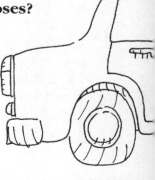

"How do you get down from an elephant?"
"I don't know. How do you get down from
an elephant?"
"You don't. You get down from a duck!"
Helen Lewis, 13, Darlington

Where does an elephant sleep?
Anywhere he wants to!
Phillip Tuckwell, 10, Derby

What do you give to
seasick elephants?
Plenty of room!
P.W. Harper, 12,
Birkenhead

Why do elephants paint the soles of their
feet yellow?
So they can hide upside down in bowls of
custard!
(Have you ever seen an elephant in a bowl
of custard?
Well then...)
Chris Quinten, Stuart Messenger and Ben Guest,
Winchester

Why did the elephant cross the road?

The chicken was on holiday!

Rupert Reed, Chelmsford

What do two elephants play in a mini?

Squash!

Imogen Dyckoff, 9, Scunthorpe

What do you get if you cross a kangaroo with a sheep and some glue?

A woolly jumper!

But what about the glue?

I thought you'd get stuck on that!

Robert Bryan, 9, Winchester

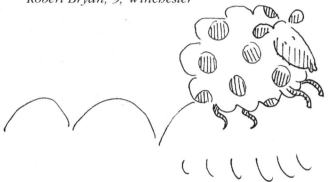

What says "Kangeroot"?

A Scotsman locked in a loo, "I canna–ger–oot"!

Ashley Orwin, 10, Sheffield

What do you get if you lie down under a cow?

A pat on the head.

Helen Brownlow, 8, Lincoln

Where do cows go on holiday?

Moo York.

Mark Follos, 7, Leicester

MACHINES

How do you sink an Irish submarine?
Knock on the door!
James Pocklington, 12, Witham Hall, Chelmsford

A fat driver had a car which broke down. The AA man came and said, "Your battery's flat," and the fat man replied, "Well what shape should it be?"
E. Burt, E. House, New Milton

Machines

**What's white, swings through the jungle
and hurts when it hits you on the head?**
A fridge!

James Steel, 15, Eversley/Staines

**I had a wooden car with wooden wheels,
wooden engine, wooden ignition, wooden
seats and it wouldn't go!**

Johannes Gascoine-Becker, 10, Bletchingley

**What did the robot say to the petrol
pump?**
Take your fingers out of you ears when I'm
talking to you!

Dean Checkley, 10, Eversfield School, Solihul

**What do you get when you cross the
Atlantic with the *Titanic*?**
Halfway!

Mark Dixon, 10, Nottingham

**A plane was flying to New Zealand. A call
from the Control Tower said, "How high
are you and what is your position?" The
pilot radioed back, "I'm six foot
tall and I'm sitting in the front
of the plane!"**

*James Needham, 9,
Eversfield School, Solihull*

☆ **What do you get if you cross a motor-bike with a kitten?**
Something that goes up the M1 going
MEEOWWW.

Bernard Cribbins

FOOD

Shall I tell you a joke about butter?

No, you'll only spread it!

James Johnstone, Wilmslow

What do you give a hurt lemon?

Lemonade!

Katie Mountford, 8, Stone

What do you get if you cross a football team with ice–cream?

Aston Villa.

Jamie Watson, 11, Glasgow

How do you make an apple puff?

Chase it round the garden!

Kelly Anthony, 11, Peterborough

Food

A man goes into a pub and asks for helicopter flavoured crisps. The landlord says, "Sorry, I've only got plain ones!"
Simon Hutton, 10, Sheffield

Why did the orange go to the doctor?
Because it wasn't peeling well!
John Ross, 11, Glasgow

What do you call a train loaded with toffees?
A chew-chew train!
Richard Hawkins, 8, Winchester

Have you heard the joke about the cornflake?
You'll have to wait - it's a cereal!
Neil Young, Chelmsford

Did you know that the law of gravity reverses when you eat school dinners? What goes down must come up!
Emma Maskell, 11, Scunthorpe

What did one grape say to the other grape?
Nothing. Grapes can't talk!
Thomas Dunn, 9, Fairfield School, Loughborough

"Waitress, there's a bone in my steak!"
"Yes sir....It helps the cow stand up!"
Robert Brown, 13, Leicester

"Waiter, waiter, my coffee tastes like mud."
"I'm not surprised sir, it's fresh ground!"
Morgan Green, 12, Princethorpe College

MEDICINE

the Xceedingly funny joke book

What's an excellent way of stopping your eyes from getting sore?
Take your spoon out of your coffee before you drink it!
Nick Hammond, 20, Scunthorpe

What can NEVER be made right?
Your left ear!
Nicola Buck, 8, Norwich

Doctor, Doctor, I feel like a snooker ball!
Please go to the end of the cue!
Erin C. Kirke, 11, Nottingham

Doctor, Doctor, I feel like a pin!
I can see your point!
Andrew Guyton, 8, Birkenhead

Patient : Doctor, Doctor....I think I'm a cricket ball!
Doctor : How's that?
Patient : Oh no, not YOU as well...
David Clarke, 10, Fairfield School, Loughborough

☆ **Doctor, Doctor, I've broken my arm in several places.**

You must stop going to these places then!

Kevin Lloyd

Did you hear about the dentist who became a brain surgeon when his drill slipped?

Charles Fleek, 11,
Bilton Grange/Coventry

Doctor, Doctor, I can't fall asleep!

Lie on the edge of the bed, you'll soon drop off!

Daniel Hunt, Oldham

Doctor, Doctor, I feel like an apple!

Well come in, I won't bite you!

Lucy Walton, 11, Peterborough

Doctor, Doctor, my child has just fallen down a well!

You should get a book on raising children.

Ryan Swindells, 11, Altrincham

☆ **Man : Doctor, Doctor, you must help me. I keep thinking I'm a dog!**

Doctor : All right, Mr. Smithson, get up on the couch.

Man : I can't, I'm not allowed on the furniture!

Nicholas Lyndhurst

EDUCATION

Teacher : "Make up a sentence with the word 'judicious' in it."
Pupil : "Hands that judicious can feel soft as your face with mild green Fairy Liquid."
A. Peart, 11, Wilmslow

What's Geometry?
It's what a tree says when it looks in the mirror, "Gee I'm a tree!"
David Vinton, Newcastle upon Tyne

Teacher ; "You should have been here at 9.15, Lucy."
Lucy : "Why, what did I miss?"
Mitchell Hargreaves, 15, Sheffield

Education

What exams do farmers' children take?
Hay Levels!
Anthony Greaves, 10, Sutton Coldfield

Teacher : "I hope I didn't see you copying Finlay's work, Paul!"
Paul : "I hope you didn't as well, Miss!"
Finlay McNab, 9, Fairfield School, Loughborough

Mum said to son, "Why are you taking your gun to school?"
Son replied, "The teacher is going to teach us how to draw."
Robert Broad, Wilmslow

Pupil to teacher :
"Sir, would you tell me off for something I haven't done?"
"No, of course not."
"Well, sir, I haven't done my homework."
James Green, 13, Coventry

John said to his mother, "I don't want to go to school today - the teachers frighten me and the kids are horrible!"
His mother said, "You've GOT to go John, you're the Headmaster!"
Lorna Rees, 8, Northampton

GHOSTS
AND
FAIRIES

What do ghosts eat for pudding?
Boo-Berry Pie!
Philippa Scott, 10, St. Martin's School, Solihull

What do ghosts have for breakfast?
Dreaded Wheat!
Alex Knight, 9, Altrincham

Where does a goblin go to keep fit?
An elf farm!
John Doughty, 10, Stone

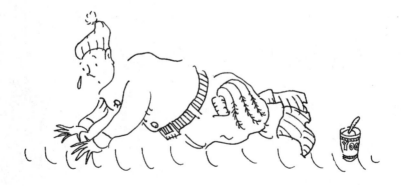

First Ghost to Second Ghost :
Do you believe in people? (Think about it!)
Matthew Collier, 10, Northampton/Coventry

Ghosts and Fairies

What happens if you put your head under the pillow?
The fairy takes all your teeth away!
Kevin Prior, Winchester,
Christopher Hartley, 11, Harrogate

Where do skeletons swim?
The Dead sea!
Sunhil Sangha, 8, Hinckley

MISCELLANEOUS

What goes at 90 miles per hour down a clothes line?
Honda Pants!
Richard Johnson, 11, Ramillies Hall, Wilmslow,
Mark Cox, 10, Scunthorpe

How do you make a band stand?
Hide all the chairs!
Andrew Williamson, 12, Stone

Which part of the horror film scared you most?
The part where I ran out of popcorn!
Crispin Jinks, 9,
St. Crispins Prep. School/Leicester

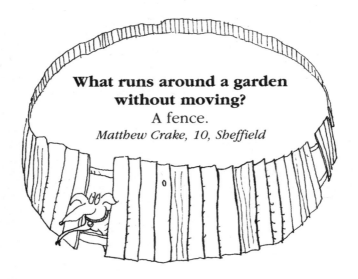

What runs around a garden without moving?
A fence.
Matthew Crake, 10, Sheffield

What happens if you put a grand piano on a battlefield?

You get A flat major!

Edmund Todd, 11, Witham Hall

the Xceedingly funny joke book

☆ **From the Secret Diary of Adrian Mole:**
"Tuesday March 9th.
Full Moon.
My schoolwork is plummeting down to new depths. I only got five out of twenty for spelling, I think I might be anorexic!"
Printed with kind permission of Sue Townsend

How many ears has Captain Kirk got?
Three - the left ear, the right ear and the final front ear!
James Houlton, 9, Tonbridge

What do you call a boomerang that won't come back?
A stick.
James Hall, Oldham,
Brennan Taylor, 10, Loughborough

How do you get rid of varnish?
Take away the letter "r"!
Ryan Pemble, 9, Tonbridge

Miscellaneous

What is an ig?
An Eskimo's house without a toilet.
Carrie Wilson, 15, Nottingham

What do you say if you go into an Egyptian house?
Toot and come in! (Think about it!)
Mark Wood, 9, Sutton Coldfield

BOOK TITLES

PARACHUTE JUMPING by Willie Maykit
RUN FOR YOUR LIVES by General Panic
NOT TOO FAST by Ann Dante
Neil Joisce, Winchester

Where do they make laws with holes in them?

The houses of Polomint!

David Williamson, Nottingham

How do you cut the sea in half ?

With a sea saw.

Fay Bishop, Chelmsford,
Andrew Gough, 10, Stone

First published 1990 by Walker Books Ltd
87 Vauxhall Walk, London SE11 5HJ

Text © 1990 Dyslexia Institute
Illustrations © 1990 Bill Piggins

This edition published 1990
Printed by Richard Clay Ltd.,
Bungay, Suffolk

British Library Cataloguing in Publication Data
The Xceedingly funny joke book.
1. Man. Dyslexia
I. Dyslexia Institute
616.85'53

ISBN 0–7445–1600–5